Poets of the First World War

JON STALLWORTHY

OXFORD UNIVERSITY PRESS
in association with the
Imperial War Museum
London, 1974

Introduction

In times of war and national calamity, large numbers of people seldom seen in church or book-shop will turn for consolation and inspiration to religion and poetry. Never was the interaction of these two more clearly demonstrated than in that war we still, many wars later, know by the adjective Great.

On Easter Sunday 1915, the Dean of St. Paul's preached in the Cathedral to a large congregation of widows, parents, and orphans. Dean Inge gave as his text *Isaiah XXVI*, 19. 'The dead shall live, my body shall arise. Awake and sing, ye that dwell in the dust.' He had just read a poem on this subject, he said, 'a sonnet by a young writer who would', he ventured to think, 'take rank with our great poets—so potent was a time of trouble to evoke genius which must otherwise have slumbered.' He then read aloud Rupert Brooke's 'The Soldier' (see page 6), and remarked that 'the expression of a pure and elevated patriotism had never found a nobler expression'. So Brooke the soldier-poet was canonized by the Church, and many other poets, soldiers and civilians alike, found inspiration for their battle hymns, elegies, exhortations, in *Hymns Ancient and Modern*:

> For a Europe's flouted laws
>   We the sword reluctant drew,
> Righteous in a righteous cause:
>   Britons, we WILL see it through!
>   (R. M. Freeman, from 'The War Cry')

or in the School Song, itself a derivative of the Anglican hymn:

> Lad, with the merry smile and the eyes
>   Quick as a hawk's and clear as the day,
> You who have counted the game the prize,
>   Here is the game of games to play.
>   Never a goal—the captains say—
> Matches the one that's needed now:
>   Put the old blazer and cap away—
> England's colours await your brow.
>   (R. E. Vernède, from 'The Call')

Hundreds of what came to be called 'war poets' saw their work in print between 1914 and 1918, and others—including some of the best—were not published until afterwards. It is an unsatisfactory label: Freeman and Vernède, for example, have little in common with Owen and Sassoon, whose poems of passionate indignation are a far cry from Edward Thomas's bleak and oblique rural ruminations.

We can now see that most of the 'war poets'—like most 'peace poets' before and since—were bad poets, but there were also a number of good poets, true poets; and 'the true Poets', wrote Wilfred Owen, 'must be truthful'. The following pages give a brief account of the life and work of six who were true to their different forms of experience. There were others: E. E. Cummings, Ford Madox Ford, Robert Graves, Julian Grenfell, Ivor Gurney, Thomas Hardy, David Jones, Rudyard Kipling, Robert Nichols, Herbert Read, Charles Hamilton Sorley. These should not be forgotten, nor should the speechless millions of whom and for whom they spoke:

> Battalions and battalions, scarred from hell;
> The unreturning army that was youth;
> The legions who have suffered and are dust.

Rupert Chawner Brooke

was born on 3 August 1887. His father was a house-master at Rugby School, and Rupert and his two brothers grew up in the comfortable security of a home dedicated to the ideals of 'godliness and good learning'. Having discovered the power of poetry —from a chance reading of Browning—at the age of nine, Rupert entered his father's school in 1901. From the start he did well both in the classroom and on the playing field; for although early on he adopted the pose of the decadent aesthete, winning the school poetry prize in 1905, he found time to play in the cricket XI and the rugger XV.

Just under six foot tall, he was strikingly hand-some, and people would turn in the street to watch him pass under a tossing mane of red-gold hair. This physical presence was matched by a sharp-ness of intellect, a charm and vitality of manner that affected everyone with whom he came into contact. Popular and successful at Rugby, he was even more so at King's College, Cambridge, where he went as a scholar in 1906. He read more voraciously than ever, he threw himself into acting (playing the parts of Mephistopheles in Marlowe's *Dr. Faustus* and the Attendant Spirit in Milton's *Comus*) and into the activities of the University Fabian Society, of which he became president. His circle of friends soon included Frances Cornford, E. M. Forster, Hugh Dalton, George Leigh Mallory, Geoffrey and Maynard Keynes, and Virginia Stephen (later to make her name as Virginia Woolf). When Henry James visited Cambridge in 1909, he too fell under the spell of the golden-haired young man who punted him down the Cam, although the pole was unfortunately allowed to fall on the Master's bald head. Told that Rupert Brooke wrote poetry, but that it was no good, he replied: 'Well, I must say I am relieved, for with that appearance if he had also talent it would be too unfair.'

Talent, however, there was. This and an un-swerving dedication to poetry were producing poems in which a modern voice was soon making itself heard through the period diction:

Dawn

(From the train between Bologna and Milan, second class)

Opposite me two Germans snore and sweat.
　　Through sullen swirling gloom we jolt and
　　　　roar.
We have been here for ever: even yet
　　A dim watch tells two hours, two æons,
　　　　more.
The windows are tight-shut and slimy-wet
　　With a night's fœtor. There are two hours
　　　　more;
Two hours to dawn and Milan; two hours yet.
　　Opposite me two Germans sweat and snore....

One of them wakes, and spits, and sleeps
    again.
  The darkness shivers. A wan light through
    the rain
Strikes on our faces, drawn and white.
    Somewhere
  A new day sprawls; and, inside, the foul air
Is chill, and damp, and fouler than before. . . .
  Opposite me two Germans sweat and snore.

Having gained a second class in the Cambridge Classical Tripos, Brooke established himself in Granchester at the Old Vicarage (afterwards made famous by his poem 'Granchester') and began to work at a dissertation on Webster and the Elizabethan dramatists. His pastoral existence, however, was interrupted by an unhappy love affair, and in 1912 he travelled through France and Germany in search of peace of mind. Partially recovered, he returned to England and was elected to a Fellowship at King's. He divided his time between Cambridge and London, where through Eddie Marsh, a prominent civil servant with literary tastes, he met such poets as Lascelles Abercrombie, Wilfrid Gibson, and John Drinkwater, and made friends in social and political circles centred on Violet Asquith, the Prime Minister's brilliant and attractive daughter.

Falling in love again, this time with the actress Cathleen Nesbitt, Brooke decided that he needed a change of scene while considering what to do with his life, and in May 1913 he sailed for America. He had been commissioned by the *Westminster Gazette* to write a series of articles on his impressions of the United States and Canada, and over the coming months sent back a dozen such dispatches. His friends received a stream of vivid, entertaining, and frequently ribald letters that showed the poet revelling in his role of Byronic self-exile. Christmas 1913 found him in New Zealand, reached by way of Hawaii, Samoa, and Fiji, and a month later he was in Tahiti. This he decided was 'the most ideal place in the world' and, finding in this Pacific paradise an Eve (called Taatamata), he wrote a number of happy poems:

Rupert Brooke in the garden of the Old Vicarage

Rupert Brooke and friends on a picnic

Taü here, Mamua,
Crown the hair, and come away!
Hear the calling of the moon,
And the whispering scents that stray
About the idle warm lagoon.
Hasten, hand in human hand,
Down the dark, the flowered way,
Along the whiteness of the sand,
And in the water's soft caress,
Wash the mind of foolishness,
Mamua, until the day.
Spend the glittering moonlight there
Pursuing down the soundless deep
Limbs that gleam and shadowy hair,
Or floating lazy, half-asleep.
Dive and double and follow after,
Snare in flowers, and kiss, and call,
With lips that fade, and human laughter
And faces individual,
Well this side of Paradise! . . .
There's little comfort in the wise.

He returned to England in June and two months later was in a music-hall when a scribbled message was thrown across the screen:

> 'War declared with Austria. 11. 9.' There was a volley of quick low handclapping—more a signal of recognition than anything else. Then we dispersed into Trafalgar Square, and bought midnight war editions, special. All these days I have not been so near tears. There was such tragedy, and such dignity, in the people.

He was commissioned into the Royal Naval Division (R.N.V.R.), and in mid October took part in its brief and abortive expedition to Antwerp. This he described in a letter to Cathleen Nesbitt:

> The sky was lit by burning villages and houses; and after a bit we got to the land by the river, where the Belgians had let all the petrol out of the tanks and fired it. Rivers and seas of

5

HOOD BATTALION,

2nd NAVAL BRIGADE,

BLANDFORD,

DORSET.

The Soldier

If I should die, think only this of me:
 That there's some corner of a foreign field
That is for ever England. There shall be
 In that rich earth a richer dust concealed;
A dust whom England bore, shaped, made aware,
 Gave, once, her flowers to love, her ways to roam,
A body of England's, breathing English air,
 Washed by the rivers, blest by suns of home.

And think, this heart, all evil shed away,
 A pulse in the eternal mind, no less
 Gives somewhere back the thoughts by England given;
Her sights and sounds; dreams happy as her day;
 And laughter, learnt of friends; and gentleness,
 In hearts at peace, under an English heaven.

flame leaping up hundreds of feet, crowned by black smoke that covered the entire heavens. It lit up houses wrecked by shells, dead horses, demolished railway stations, engines that had been taken up with their lines and signals, and all twisted round and pulled out, as a bad child spoils a toy. And there we joined the refugees, with all their goods on barrows and carts, in a double line, moving forwards about a hundred yards an hour, white and drawn and beyond emotion. The glare was like hell. We passed on, out of that, across a pontoon bridge, built on boats. Two German spies tried to blow it up while we were on it. They were caught and shot. We went on through the dark. The refugees and motor-buses and transport and Belgian troops grew thicker. After about a thousand years it was dawn.

On leave in December he wrote the five War Sonnets that were to make him famous—'Peace', 'Safety', two called 'The Dead', and 'The Soldier' —and on 1 March embarked with the Hood Battalion on a troopship destined (though they did not know it) for Gallipoli. On the voyage Brooke contracted first heatstroke, then dysentery, and finally bloodpoisoning, of which he died on 23 April. That evening he was buried on the Greek island of Skyros.

England at this time needed a focal point for its griefs, ideals, and aspirations, and the Valediction that appeared in *The Times* over the initials of Winston Churchill, the First Lord of the Admiralty, sounded a note that was to swell over the months and years that followed:

> The thoughts to which he gave expression in the very few incomparable war sonnets which he has left behind will be shared by many thousands of young men moving resolutely and blithely forward into this, the hardest, the cruellest, and the least-rewarded of all the wars that men have fought. They are a whole history and revelation of Rupert Brooke himself. Joyous,

fearless, versatile, deeply instructed, with classic symmetry of mind and body, he was all that one would wish England's noblest sons to be in days when no sacrifice but the most precious is acceptable, and the most precious is that which is most freely proffered.

Brooke's *1914 and Other Poems* was published in June 1915 and over the next decade this and his *Collected Poems* sold 300,000 copies.

He has sometimes been criticized for not responding to the horrors of war, but it should be remembered that in 1914 Wilfred Owen was himself writing:

> O meet it is and passing sweet
>   To live in peace with others,
> But sweeter still and far more meet,
>   To die in war for brothers.

Had Brooke lived to experience the Gallipoli landings or the trenches of the Western Front, it is hard to imagine that the poet of 'Dawn' (see above) would not have written as realistically as Owen and Sassoon.

Edmund Charles Blunden

was born in London on 1 November 1896 and two years later moved with his family to a village in Kent where his father was a schoolmaster. From the local grammar school Blunden won a scholarship to Christ's Hospital, Horsham, where in due course he became senior 'Grecian'. He was happy at school and was to remain devoted to it all his life. Coleridge, Leigh Hunt, and Lamb had walked its corridors and sat at its benches, and the writings of these 'Old Blues' were a major influence on the young poet. In 1914 he gained the senior classics scholarship at Queen's College, Oxford, and privately printed two pamphlets of verse: *Poems* and *Poems Translated from the French*.

The outbreak of war changed his life like that of so many others. Within months he was training as a volunteer with the Royal Sussex Regiment and in 1916, a temporary 2nd lieutenant, he crossed to France. His initiation at the Etaples Base Camp (known to thousands of British soldiers as Eat-apples or Heeltaps) was a violent foretaste of experiences to come.

Rifle-grenade instruction began. A Highland sergeant-major stood magnificently before us, with the brass brutality called a Hales rifle-grenade in his hand. He explained the piece, fingering the wind-vane with easy assurance; then stooping to the fixed rifle, he prepared to shoot the grenade by way of demonstration. According to my unsoldierlike habit, I had let the other students press near the instructor, and was listlessly standing on the skirts of the meeting, thinking of something else, when the sergeant-major having just said 'I've been down here since 1914, and never had an accident', there was a strange hideous clang. Several voices cried out; I found myself stretched on the floor, looking upwards in the delusion that the grenade had been fired straight above and was about to fall among us. It had indeed been fired, but by some error had burst at the muzzle of the rifle: the instructor was lying with mangled head, dead, and others lay near him, also blood-masked, dead and alive.

A day or two later he was on his way to the Front and was soon under fire in the Old British Line on the outskirts of the village of Festubert.

At some points in the trench, bones pierced through their shallow burial, and skulls appeared like mushrooms. The men with whom I was now consorted instantly appeared good men, shy, quiet, humorous, and neat. The sandbag walls did not look so mighty as the night before, but still I thought that they must be able to withstand a great deal. Limbery-Buse thought not. As I look back on those breastworks, very often single walls, with no protection at all against the back-blast of shells, with their wooden fire-steps, their roofings of corrugated iron or old doors, I am of his opinion; and even that first morning I might have known; for the howling and whooping of shells suddenly began, and a small brick outbuilding between our trench and Festubert village behind began to jump away in explosions of dusty yellow smoke. . . .

We were well off in this reserve trench, though my blood ran high in the excitement of novelty. In the evenings, while some of the men were amusing themselves in digging out a colony of rats, for which sport they had enlisted a stray terrier, there would suddenly begin a tremendous upheaval two or three miles to the south. The officers not on definite duty would leave their dinner to stand and terrify their eyes with this violence. On the blue and lulling mist of evening, proper to the nightingale, the sheepbell, and falling waters, the strangest phenomena of fire inflicted themselves. The red sparks of German trench mortars described their seeming-slow arcs, shrapnel shells clanged in crimson, burning, momentary cloudlets, smoke billowed into a tidal wave, and the powdery glare of many a signal-light showed the rolling folds.

These quotations from Blunden's *Undertones of War* (1929) reveal much of the man: skulls protruding from the trench-wall remind him of mushrooms, the flashes of the guns reveal 'the blue and lulling mist of evening, proper to the nightingale, the sheepbell, and falling waters'. He described himself as 'a harmless young shepherd in a soldier's coat' and he sees the battlefield with a countryman's eye. There is a countryman's tender delight in all living things and a corresponding

PILLBOX

Just see what's happening, Worley!   Worley rose
And round the angled doorway thrust his nose
And Serjeant Hyde went too to snuff the air.
Then war brought down his fist, and missed the pair!
Yet Hyde was hit by a splinter, the blood came,
And out sprang terrors that he'd striven to tame,
A good man, Hyde, for weeks. I'm blown to bits,
He screams, he screams.   Come Bluffer, where's your wits,
Says Worley, Bluffer, you've a blighty, man!
All in the pillbox urged him, here began
His freedom: Think of Eastbourne and your dad,
The poor man lay at length and brief and mad
Flung out his cry of doom; soon ebbed and dumb
He yielded. Worley with a tot of rum
And shouting in his face could not restore him,
The ship of Charon over channel bore him,
All marvelled even on that most deathly day
To see this soul so spirited away.

Edmund Blunden

sense of outrage at the mutilations of war. The countryman's eye, however, is at the service of a highly sophisticated literary intelligence. Although only twenty years old when he entered the trenches, he was already steeped in English literature, and in his war poems married the language of Keats and Shakespeare and Spenser with the harsher diction of the day.

Vlamertinghe

Passing the Château, July 1917

'And all her silken flanks with garlands drest'—
But we are coming to the sacrifice.
Must those have flowers who are not yet gone
   West?
May those have flowers who live with death
   and lice?
This must be the floweriest place
That earth allows; the queenly face
Of the proud mansion borrows grace for grace
Spite of those brute guns lowing at the skies.

Bold great daisies' golden lights,
Bubbling roses' pinks and whites—
Such a gay carpet! poppies by the million;
Such damask! such vermilion!
But if you ask me, mate, the choice of colour
Is scarcely right: this red should have been
   duller.

He begins this poem with a quotation from Keats's 'Ode on a Grecian Urn' and ends it with a soldier's colloquialism.

With his Regiment, to which he was ever afterwards to remain deeply attached, Blunden went through the horrors of Cuinchy Brickstacks and Thiepval Wood, and in 1917 was awarded the Military Cross. Miraculously, he survived unscathed, although memories of the War were to haunt him for the rest of his life and leave marks on his imagination revealed in such later poems as 'Pike', 'The Midnight Skaters', and 'Report on Experience'. The last of these records experiences that would have embittered a man less firmly rooted in a basic optimism and a belief in the essential goodness of life:

I have seen a green country, useful to the race,
Knocked silly with guns and mines, its villages
   vanished,
Even the last rat and last kestrel banished—
   God bless us all, this was peculiar grace.

I knew Seraphina; Nature gave her hue,
Glance, sympathy, note, like one from Eden.
I saw her smile warp, heard her lyric deaden;
   She turned to harlotry;—this I took to be
   new.

Say what you will, our God sees how they run.
These disillusions are his curious proving
That he loves humanity and will go on loving;
   Over there are faith, life, virtue in the sun.

After demobilization in 1919, Blunden took up his scholarship at Oxford, and was subsequently at different times a journalist, Professor of English in the University of Tokyo, Fellow and Tutor at Merton College, Oxford, cultural Liaison Officer to the British Mission in Japan, and Professor of Poetry at Oxford. He wrote several volumes of poems and critical or biographical studies of a wide range of English authors: among them, Hardy, Coleridge, Shelley, and Keats. Wherever he went he was loved and respected for his learning, his wisdom, his modesty, his humour, and his generosity. The last was legendary and extended not only to the living but the dead, such as John Clare and Wilfred Owen, whose poems he edited with rare devotion.

He died in 1974 and went to his grave in a coffin on which one of his old comrades had laid a wreath of Flanders poppies.

Wilfred Edward Salter Owen

was born in Oswestry on 18 March 1893. His parents were then living in a spacious and comfortable house owned by his grandfather, Edward Shaw. At his death two years later, this former Mayor of the city was found to be almost bankrupt, and Tom Owen was obliged to move with his wife and son to lodgings in the backstreets of Birkenhead. They carried with them vivid memories of their vanished prosperity, and Susan Owen resolved that her adored son Wilfred should in time restore the family to its rightful gentility. She was a devout lady and under her strong influence Wilfred grew into a serious and slightly priggish boy. At school in Birkenhead and later in Shrewsbury—where Tom Owen was appointed Assistant Superintendent of the Joint Railways (GWR and LNWR) in 1906—he worked hard and successfully, especially at literature and botany. He had begun writing poems when he was ten or eleven, and soon fell under the spell of Keats, who was to remain the principal influence on his work.

Leaving school in 1911, Owen took up a post as lay assistant to the Vicar of Dunsden in Oxfordshire. He was to help the Vicar with his parish work and receive in return coaching for the university entrance examination that he hoped in due course to sit. Removed from his mother's influence, he became less enamoured of evangelical religion and more critical of the role of the Church—as represented by the Vicar of Dunsden—in society. His letters and poems of this period show an increasing awareness of the sufferings of the poor and the first stirrings of the compassion that was to characterize his later poems about the Western Front. He attended botany classes at Reading University and was encouraged by the Professor of English to read and write more poetry. In February 1913, on the verge of a nervous breakdown, he left Dunsden and, when he had recovered, crossed to France where he taught at the Berlitz School of Languages in Bordeaux.

He was in the Pyrenees, acting as tutor in a cultivated French household, when war was declared. A visit to a hospital for the wounded soon opened his eyes to the true nature of war, but it was not until September 1915 that he finally decided to return to England and enlist. For several months he and Edward Thomas were privates, training at Hare Hall Camp in Essex, but there is no evidence that they ever met. Commissioned into the Manchester Regiment, Owen crossed the Channel on 30 December 1916 and in the first days of January joined the 2nd Manchesters on the Somme near Beaumont Hamel. His letters to his mother tell their own story:

> I have not been at the front.
> I have been in front of it.
> I held an advanced post, that is, a 'dug-out' in the middle of No Man's Land.

A Manchester Regiment working party, January 1917

We had a march of 3 miles over shelled road then nearly 3 along a flooded trench. After that we came to where the trenches had been blown flat out and had to go over the top. It was of course dark, too dark, and the ground was not mud, not sloppy mud, but an octopus of sucking clay, 3, 4, and 5 feet deep, relieved only by craters full of water. Men have been known to drown in them. Many stuck in the mud and only got on by leaving their waders, equipment, and in some cases their clothes.

High explosives were dropping all around us, and machine guns spluttered every few minutes. But it was so dark that even the German flares did not reveal us.

Three quarters dead, I mean each of us $\frac{3}{4}$ dead, we reached the dug-out, and relieved the wretches therein. I then had to go forth and find another dug-out for a still more advanced post where I left 18 bombers. I was responsible for

other posts on the left but there was a junior officer in charge.

My dug-out held 25 men tight packed. Water filled it to a depth of 1 or 2 feet, leaving say 4 feet of air.

One entrance had been blown in and blocked. So far, the other remained.

The Germans knew we were staying there and decided we shouldn't.

Those fifty hours were the agony of my happy life.

Every ten minutes on Sunday afternoon seemed an hour.

I nearly broke down and let myself drown in the water that was now slowly rising over my knees.

Towards 6 o'clock, when, I suppose, you would be going to church, the shelling grew less intense and less accurate: so that I was mercifully helped to do my duty and crawl, wade,

14

climb and flounder over No Man's Land to visit my other post. It took me half an hour to move about 150 yards.

I was chiefly annoyed by our own machine guns from behind. The seeng-seeng-seeng of the bullets reminded me of Mary's canary. On the whole I can support the canary better.

In the Platoon on my left the sentries over the dug-out were blown to nothing. One of these poor fellows was my first servant whom I rejected. If I had kept him he would have lived, for servants don't do Sentry Duty. I kept my own sentries half way down the stairs during the more terrific bombardment. In spite of this one lad was blown down and, I am afraid, blinded.

That last experience was to find its way into Owen's poem 'The Sentry', more than a year and a half later.

In March 1917 he fell into a cellar and suffered concussion, and some weeks later, after fierce fighting near St. Quentin, was invalided home with shell-shock. At Craiglockhart War Hospital on the outskirts of Edinburgh he met Siegfried Sassoon, whose first 'war poems' had just appeared in *The Old Huntsman and Other Poems*. Under their influence and with the encouragement and guidance of the older poet, Owen was soon producing poems far superior to any he had written previously: 'The Next War', 'Anthem for Doomed Youth', 'Disabled', and 'Dulce et Decorum Est'. Sassoon not only helped him to purge his style of its early excessive luxuriance, but introduced him to such other poets and novelists as Robert Graves, Arnold Bennett, H. G. Wells, and Osbert Sitwell.

Discharged from Craiglockhart in October, Owen was posted to the 5th Manchesters in Scarborough and there wrote 'The Show' and probably 'Exposure' and 'Strange Meeting'. In March 1918 he was transferred to Ripon. 'The Send-Off',

Distant view of St. Quentin from the British front line trench, April 1917

Anthem for Doomed Youth —   Nation

What passing-bells for these who die as cattle?
    — Only the monstrous anger of the guns.
      Only the stuttering rifles' rapid rattle
Can patter out their hasty orisons.
No {music for all them} {nor no} {prayers nor bells}
   {mockeries} for them; {from} prayers {or bells}
      Nor any voice of mourning save the choirs,
The shrill demented choirs of wailing shells;
And bugles calling sad across the shires.
              for them from sad

What candles may be held to speed them all?
    Not in the hands of boys, but in their eyes
Shall shine the holy glimmers of goodbyes.
The pallor of girls' brows shall be their pall;
Their flowers the tenderness of {silent patient} minds;
And each slow dusk a drawing-down of blinds.

Final draft of 'Anthem for Doomed Youth'. At the foot of this manuscript there is a note in Siegfried Sassoon's hand: 'Pencil words were written by S.S. when W. showed him the sonnet at Craiglockhart in Sept. 1917.'

written at this period, is typical of his later work in the way it makes its bitter statement with brilliant economy, its calm surface mined with ironies:

The Send-Off

Down the close darkening lanes they sang
  their way
To the siding-shed,
And lined the train with faces grimly gay.

Their breasts were stuck all white with wreath
  and spray
As men's are, dead.

Dull porters watched them, and a casual tramp
Stood staring hard,
Sorry to miss them from the upland camp.

Then, unmoved, signals nodded, and a lamp
Winked to the guard.

So secretly, like wrongs hushed-up, they went.
They were not ours:
We never heard to which front these were sent.

Nor there if they yet mock what women meant
Who gave them flowers.

Shall they return to beatings of great bells
In wild train-loads?
A few, a few, too few for drums and yells,

May creep back, silent, to still village wells
Up half-known roads.

At the end of August Owen was certified 'fit to proceed overseas' and, a month later, was again in action. He was awarded the Military Cross for his part in a successful attack on the Beaurevoir-Fonsomme Line and, before sunrise on the morning of 4 November, led his platoon to the west bank of the Sambre and Oise Canal. They came under murderous fire from German machine guns behind the parapet of the east bank, and at the height of the ensuing battle Owen was hit and killed while helping his men bring up duck-boards at the water's edge.

In Shrewsbury, the Armistice bells were ringing when his parents' front-door bell sounded its small chime, heralding the telegram they had dreaded for two years.

The Sambre and Oise Canal, November 1918

Isaac Rosenberg

was born in Bristol on 25 November 1890. His parents had emigrated from Russia some years before. When he was seven, the family moved to the East End of London in search of better-paid work, but they were not successful and the boy, whose health had never been good, developed a lung ailment. From the Board School of St. George's in the East he went on to Stepney Board School, where his natural gift for drawing and for writing so impressed the headmaster that he allowed him to spend most of his time on them. Out of school, he used to read poetry and draw with chalks on the pavements of the East End.

Obliged to leave school at fourteen, he was apprenticed to the firm of Carl Hertschel, engravers, in Fleet Street. His parents hoped that this might prove a stepping-stone to a painter's career, but Isaac hated the work, writing in a letter: 'It is horrible to think that all these hours, when my days are full of vigour and my hands craving for self-expression, I am bound, chained to this fiendish mangling machine, without hope and almost desire of deliverance'. He wrote poems in his lunch-hours, and in the evenings attended classes in the Art School of Birkbeck College. At last, his apprenticeship completed, he was free and in 1911 three generous Jewish women undertook to pay his tuition fees at the Slade School of Fine Art. There he came to know the painters Gertler, Bomberg, Kramer, Roberts, Nevinson, and Stanley Spencer, but increasingly found art and poetry incompatible and himself drawn towards poetry. 'Art is not a plaything', he wrote, 'it is blood and tears, it must grow up with one; and I believe I have begun too late'. Even so, he was a capable draughtsman and painted some good pictures, a few of which were exhibited at the Whitechapel Gallery. Leaving the Slade, he considered going to Russia, but it was difficult for a Jew to get a passport and he abandoned the idea. He had hoped to earn a living from his portraits, but in 1914 was told that his lungs were weak and advised to seek a warmer climate. Having a married sister in Cape Town, he sailed for South Africa in June. There he painted some pictures, gave a series of lectures on modern art, and published a few articles and poems, but he was far from happy, as he made clear in a letter to Eddie Marsh:

> I am in an infernal city by the sea. This city has men in it—and these men have souls in them—or at least have the passages to souls. Though they are millions of years behind time, they have yet reached the stage of evolution that knows ears and eyes. But these passages are dreadfully clogged up: gold dust, diamond dust, stocks and shares, and Heaven knows what other flinty muck.

His reactions to the outbreak of war were complex and found their way into a poem:

On Receiving News of the War
(Cape Town, 1914)

Snow is a strange white word.
No ice or frost
Has asked of bud or bird
For Winter's cost.

Yet ice and frost and snow
From earth to sky
This Summer land doth know.
No man knows why.

In all men's hearts it is.
Some spirit old
Hath turned with malign kiss
Our lives to mould.

Red fangs have torn His face.
God's blood is shed.
He mourns from His lone place
His children dead.

O ancient crimson curse!
Corrode, consume.
Give back this universe
Its pristine bloom.

He perceives the approaching violence more distinctly than many other poets; it is an 'ancient crimson curse', but he hopes it may have a purging effect and restore the universe to its original pre-lapsarian innocence and beauty.

In 1915 he returned to England where he published a small pamphlet of poems, *Youth*, and in November or early December, enlisted in the Bantam Regiment; being, as he said, 'too short for any other'. From the first he hated the army, and the army in the person of his 'impudent schoolboy pup' of an officer disliked him. The Rosenbergs were 'Tolstoyans' and Isaac, himself the most vulnerable of men, hated the idea of killing. However, after a period of training at Bury St. Edmunds and at Farnborough, he crossed the Channel early in 1916 with the King's Own Royal Lancaster Regiment. He had not been long at the Front when he sent Eddie Marsh 'a poem I wrote in the trenches, which is surely as simple as ordinary talk':

Break of Day in the Trenches

The darkness crumbles away—
It is the same old druid Time as ever.
Only a live thing leaps my hand—
A queer sardonic rat—
As I pull the parapet's poppy
To stick behind my ear.

Droll rat, they would shoot you if they knew
Your cosmopolitan sympathies.
Now you have touched this English hand
You will do the same to a German—
Soon, no doubt, if it be your pleasure
To cross the sleeping green between.
It seems you inwardly grin as you pass
Strong eyes, fine limbs, haughty athletes
Less chanced than you for life,
Bonds to the whims of murder,
Sprawled in the bowels of the earth,
The torn fields of France.
What do you see in our eyes
At the shrieking iron and flame
Hurled through still heavens?
What quaver—what heart aghast?
Poppies whose roots are in man's veins
Drop, and are ever dropping;
But mine in my ear is safe,
Just a little white with the dust.

This address to the 'sardonic rat', who dares to
fraternize with the enemy as the soldiers themselves do not, brilliantly evokes both the horror
and the absurdity of war. In this and such other
'Poems from Camp and Trench' as 'Returning, we
Hear the Larks' and 'Dead Man's Dump', Rosenberg succeeded in his intention of writing 'Simple
poetry,—that is where an interesting complexity of
thought is kept in tone and right value to the
dominating idea so that it is understandable and
still ungraspable.'

On 28 March 1918 he ended a letter to Eddie
Marsh:

> I think I wrote you I was about to go up the
> line again after our little rest. We are now in the
> trenches again, and though I feel very sleepy, I
> just have a chance to answer your letter, so I will
> while I may. It's really my being lucky enough
> to bag an inch of candle that incites me to this
> pitch of punctual epistolary. I must measure my
> letter by the light. . . .

Before this letter was postmarked 2 April, Isaac
Rosenberg was dead.

Girl to soldier on leave.

I love you - Titan lover,
My own storm-days titan,
Greater than the son of Zeus,
I know who I would choose.

Titan - my splendid rebel -
The old Prometheus
Wanes like a ghost before your power -
His pangs were joys to yours,

Pallid days arid & wan
Tied your soul fast,
Babel cities smoky tops
Pressed upon your growth.

Weary gyves. What were you,
But a word in the brain's ways,
Or the sleep of Circe's swine.
One gyve holds you yet. -

It held you hiddenly on the Somme
Tied from my heart at home.
O must it loosen now? I wish
You were bound with the old old gyves.

Love! you love me - your eyes
Have looked through death at mine.
You have tempted a grave too much
I let you - I repine,

Siegfried Sassoon

was born on 8 September 1886. Descended from those 'jewelled merchant ancestors', the Banker Sassoons, he was brought up by his mother; his father having left his wife when his son was five. The dominant domestic presences of his childhood and youth were female: his nanny, his grandmother, the elegant socialite Mrs. Sassoon, and a regiment of devoted domestics. When he was old enough to go to Marlborough, he shuttled between all-male and all-female worlds, and grew up with the constricted emotions, the well-bred

reserve of his class. Cambridge and the History Tripos did not appeal to him and he left without taking a degree.

There being no pressure on him to choose a career or earn a living, Sassoon spent his days in the saddle or on the golf-links; his evenings at the ballet, the opera, or his London club. From 1906, when he published his first, privately-printed *Poems*, he began to move in literary circles and by August 1914 was acquainted with writers like Edmund Gosse and Eddie Marsh, Rupert Brooke and W. H. Davies. As if in acknowledgement of some subconscious need for more demanding employment, he had himself medically examined for the Army on 1 August 1914 and was wearing his ill-fitting khaki on the first morning of the Great War. He fought at Mametz Wood and in the Somme Offensive of July 1916 with such conspicuous gallantry that he acquired the Military Cross and a nickname, Mad Jack. However, invalided back to England at the beginning of April 1917, with a sniper's bullet through his chest, he began to take a different view of the War. On the lawns of

The Military Cross

Garsington Manor he met and mingled with such of Lady Ottoline Morrell's pacifist intellectual friends as Bertrand Russell and Henry Massingham, editor of *The Nation*. Influenced by them, and with courage equal to any he had shown in action, he made public a statement sent to his commanding officer.

I am making this statement as an act of wilful defiance of military authority, because I believe that the war is being deliberately prolonged by those who have the power to end it.

I am a soldier, convinced that I am acting on behalf of soldiers. I believe that this war, upon which I entered as a war of defence and liberation, has now become a war of aggression and conquest. I believe that the purposes for which

I and my fellow-soldiers entered upon this war should have been so clearly stated as to have made it impossible to change them, and that, had this been done, the objects which actuated us would now be attainable by negotiation.

I have seen and endured the sufferings of the troops, and I can no longer be a party to prolong these sufferings for ends which I believe to be evil and unjust.

I am not protesting against the conduct of the war, but against the political errors and insincerities for which the fighting men are being sacrificed.

On behalf of those who are suffering now I make this protest against the deception which is being practised on them; also I believe that I may help to destroy the callous complacence with which the majority of those at home regard

Mametz Wood

the continuance of agonies which they do not share, and which they have not sufficient imagination to realise.

Although, to a certain extent, this 'act of wilful defiance' was successful, in that it formed the subject of a question asked in the House of Commons and received an airing—a hot airing—in the press, Sassoon's protest was eventually smothered. His friend Robert Graves made urgent representations to the military authorities, as well as to certain influential civilians, that Sassoon 'should not be allowed to become a martyr to a hopeless cause in his present physical condition'. The War Office was only too glad of an opportunity to hush matters up. A Medical Board was hastily convened and rigged: 2nd Lieutenant Graves testified that his friend—who by now had thrown his Military Cross into the Mersey—suffered from hallucinations of a corpse-strewn Piccadilly and other such symptoms of shell-shock. Three times while giving his statement Graves burst into tears. The Board duly found 2nd Lieutenant Sassoon in need of medical attention and he was dispatched to Craiglockhart War Hospital.

His book, *The Old Huntsman and Other Poems*, had just appeared and it marks his abrupt transition from innocence to experience. A group of lyrical-pastoral poems (mostly written in somewhat literary language before the War) make a fierce contrast with a poem like

'They'

The Bishop tells us: 'When the boys come
  back
'They will not be the same; for they'll have
  fought
'In a just cause: they lead the last attack
'On Anti-Christ; their comrades' blood has
  bought
'New right to breed an honourable race,
'They have challenged Death and dared him
  face to face.'

'We're none of us the same!' the boys reply.
'For George lost both his legs; and Bill's
  stone blind;
'Poor Jim's shot through the lungs and like to
  die;
'And Bert's gone syphilitic: you'll not find
'A chap who's served that hasn't found *some*
  change.'
And the Bishop said: 'The ways of God are
  strange!'

With masterly use of direct speech—learnt from Thomas Hardy, to whom *The Old Huntsman* is dedicated—Sassoon attacks the hypocrisy of the Church, as in *Counter-Attack and Other Poems* (1918) he was to condemn the staff-officers' callous incompetence:

Base Details

If I were fierce, and bald, and short of breath,
  I'd live with scarlet Majors at the Base,
And speed glum heroes up the line to death.
  You'd see me with my puffy petulant face,
Guzzling and gulping in the best hotel,
  Reading the Roll of Honour. 'Poor young
  chap,'
I'd say—'I used to know his father well;
  Yes, we've lost heavily in this last scrap.'
And when the war is done and youth stone dead,
  I'd toddle safely home and die—in bed.

Leaving Craiglockhart early in 1918, Sassoon decided that he could make his protest more effectively from the Front and, after a brief tour of duty in Palestine, rejoined his battalion in France. On 13 July, returning from a dawn patrol, he was mistaken for a German and shot by one of his own N.C.O.s. He survived, however, to produce memoirs of the War and of his childhood in a more pastoral England which that War had destroyed—*The Memoirs of a Fox-hunting Man*, *The Old Country*, *The Weald of Youth*, *Memoirs of an*

The Dug-Out.

Why do you lie with your legs ungainly huddled,
And one arm bent across your sullen cold
Exhausted face? It hurts my heart to watch you,
Deep-shadow'd from the candle's guttering gold;
And you wonder why I shake you by the shoulder;
Drowsy, you mumble and sigh and turn your head...
You are too young to fall asleep for ever;
And when you sleep you remind me of the dead.

August : 1918.

Infantry Officer, *Sherston's Progress*, and *Siegfried's Journey*—that are marvels of autobiographical prose and introduced him to a wider audience than ever read his poems.

He continued to write poetry, but his style altered after the 1914–18 War. At times, as in his *Satirical Poems* (1926) attacking society, his work still displayed a cutting edge, but never again did he achieve the pungency of the 'war poems' that made him famous. In 1957 he was received into the Roman Catholic Church, and until he died in 1967 wrote mainly devotional poems. These have a calm strength that demonstrates how complete and successful was his conversion. Always a spiritual man—even when in his thirties he had attacked the Church for what he saw as its cant and hypocrisy—he found at the last a certainty and happiness not known before. As he wrote in 'Human Bondage':

> I know a universe beyond me;
> Power that pervades the fluctuant soul,
> Signalling my brain it would unbond me
> And make heart's imperfection whole.

Philip Edward Thomas

was born at Lambeth on 3 March 1878 and spent most of his childhood in London where his father was a staff clerk in the Board of Trade. A stern man, who had worked his way up in the world, he had temperamentally little in common with Edward, the oldest of his six sons. 'Almost as soon as I could babble,' the poet was later to write, 'I "babbled of green fields"', and he was never happier than in his school holidays spent with his aunt or grandmother in Swindon. There he discovered his lifelong passion for the countryside and its creatures, for country people and country pursuits.

His father introduced him to literature, first of all to the prose writers who celebrated the country and its ways, Isaac Walton and Richard Jefferies, and when he was fifteen he began to read poetry for pleasure. By then he was at St. Paul's School, Hammersmith, where his natural shyness was increased by the greater confidence of the other boys, who for the most part came from more prosperous middle-class homes. He had recently begun writing seriously—in the manner of Richard Jefferies—and found an ally and encourager in James Ashcroft Noble, a fifty-year-old journalist and author. Thomas left St. Paul's in 1895 and went up to Oxford, after two years ostensibly reading for the Civil Service examination, but in fact extending his knowledge of literature and writing a book of his own, *The Woodland Life* (1897). This was dedicated to Noble, who had died the previous year, and to whose daughter Helen he was secretly engaged. In 1899, following a courtship movingly described in her *As it Was*, they were married—secretly because of the disapproval of their parents. A year later, with a second-class degree, a baby son, and high literary ambitions, Edward Thomas left Oxford for slum lodgings in Earlsfield.

Reviewing and literary journalism were hard to find and, when found, exhausting and poorly paid. 'I now live—if living it may be called—by my writing', he told a friend, ' "literature" we call it in Fleet Street (derived from 'litter'). . . . It's a painful business, and living in this labyrinth of red brick makes it worse.' Unable to resist the lure of the country, the Thomases in 1901 moved to Kent. Their spirits rose only to be dashed by the discovery that Helen was again pregnant. She wrote: 'it means more anxiety for Edward and more work for him. Home will become unendurable to him. Even now poverty, anxiety, physical weakness, disappointments and discouragements are making him bitter, hard and impatient, quick to violent anger, and subject to long fits of depression'.

A melancholy inherited from his much-loved mother became more marked over the difficult years that followed. He was reviewing up to fifteen books a week and, though he hated the drudgery, reviewing them conscientiously and with discernment. The meagre income that brought him he supplemented by selling his review copies and writing one book after another. Thirty were published between 1897 and 1917, and during those twenty years he also edited sixteen anthologies and editions. Everything was done hurriedly, but nothing was slovenly, and he was able to find delight—and communicate it with freshness and charm—in even the most unpromising 'hack' assignment.

His great gifts as a literary critic appeared to best advantage in his reviewing of poetry, and he was the first to salute such new stars in the literary firmament as W. H. Davies the 'Super-Tramp', Robert Frost, and Ezra Pound. Coming up to London, usually in search of work—a search that with his proud modesty he hated—he met many of the leading writers of the day: Edward Garnett, Hilaire Belloc, John Masefield, Joseph Conrad, Walter de la Mare, Rupert Brooke, and D. H. Lawrence.

Though he had been reviewing poetry, which he regarded as the highest form of literature, for years, he would seem to have made no serious attempt to write it himself until autumn 1914. Then, under the stress of deciding whether or not to enlist, poems suddenly began to pour from his pen: 'Up in the Wind', 'November', 'March', 'Old Man', and 'The Sign-Post' between 3 and 7 December, and at least five more before the end of the month. On New Year's Day 1915 he sprained his ankle so badly that he was lame for nearly three months, during which time the stream of poetry flowed more swiftly and more richly than ever. From 7 to 9 January, for example, he wrote 'A Private', 'Snow', 'Adlestrop', 'Tears', and 'Over the Hills'.

While his ankle was recovering he considered emigrating to America, where his friend Robert Frost had offered to find him work, but decided against it and in July 1915 enlisted in the Artists' Rifles. A responsible family man of thirty-seven, he was much older than most of his fellow recruits and his greater maturity was soon recognized by the award of a lance-corporal's stripe. In the intervals between drilling, weapon training, clean-ing his equipment, and instructing a squad in map-reading, he was still writing poems. One of the best of them, 'Rain', illustrates a common and curious feature of his work:

Rain, midnight rain, nothing but the wild rain
On this bleak hut, and solitude, and me
Remembering again that I shall die
And neither hear the rain nor give it thanks
For washing me cleaner than I have been
Since I was born into this solitude.
Blessed are the dead that the rain rains upon:
But here I pray that none whom once I loved
Is dying tonight or lying still awake
Solitary, listening to the rain,
Either in pain or thus in sympathy
Helpless among the living and the dead,
Like a cold water among broken reeds,
Myriads of broken reeds all still and stiff,
Like me who have no love which this wild rain
Has not dissolved except the love of death,
If love it be for what is perfect and
Cannot, the tempest tells me, disappoint.

Three years before, in his prose book *The Icknield Way*, he had written

I am alone in the dark still night, and my ear listens to the rain piping in the gutters and roaring softly in the trees of the world. Even so will the rain fall darkly upon the grass over the grave when my ears can hear it no more. I have been glad of the sound of rain, and wildly sad of it in the past; but that is all over as if it had never been; my eye is dull and my heart beating evenly and quietly; I stir neither foot nor hand; I shall not be quieter when I lie under the wet grass and the rain falls, and I of less account than the grass. . . .

Black and monotonously sounding is the midnight and solitude of the rain. In a little while or in an age—for it is all one—I shall know the full truth of the words I used to love, I knew not why, in my days of nature, in the days before the rain: 'Blessed are the dead that the rain rains on.'

Steep 26 XII 15

168

This is no case of petty right or wrong
That politicians or philosophers
Can judge. I hate not Germans, nor grow hot
With love of Englishmen, to please newspapers.
Beside my hate for one fat patriot
My hatred of the Kaiser is love true:—
A kind of God he is, banging a gong.
But I have not to choose between the two,
Or between justice & injustice. Dinned
With war & argument I read no more
Than in the storm smoking along the wind
Athwart the wood. Two witches' cauldrons roar.
From one the weather shall rise clear & gay:
Out of the other an England beautiful
And like her mother that died yesterday.
Little I know or care if, being dull,
I shall miss something that historians
Can rake out of the ashes when perchance
The Phœnix broods serene above their ken.
But with the best & meanest Englishmen
I am one in crying, God save England, lest
We lose what never slaves & cattle blessed.
The ages made her that made us from dust:
She is all we know & live by, & we trust
She is good & must endure, loving her so:
And as we love ourselves we hate her foe.

His deepest loyalties and preoccupations, his love of England and her seasons celebrated so long in prose, rise again distilled to a purer form in his poems. His awareness of the natural world, its richness and beauty, is now intensified by a sense of impending loss and the certainty of death—his own and others. Thomas's 'war poems' are those of a countryman perceiving the violence done by a distant conflict to the natural order of things:

In Memoriam (Easter, 1915)

The flowers left thick at nightfall in the wood
This Eastertide call into mind the men,
Now far from home, who, with their sweet-
    hearts, should
Have gathered them and will do never again.

In January 1917, the countryman was called to the Front and, on 9 February, reached Arras, where a massive build-up for the Easter offensive was in progress. There he heard that three of his poems had been accepted by the magazine *Poetry* and, on 4 April, was heartened to read an enthusiastic review in the *Times Literary Supplement* of his contribution to *An Annual of New Poetry*. Five days later, Easter Monday, the Battle of Arras began with a deafening artillery barrage, and in the opening minutes, in a forward observation post, Edward Thomas was killed by the blast of a shell.

Further Reading

General

ANTHOLOGIES

Brian Gardner, ed., *Up the Line to Death: The War Poets, 1914–1918*, London, 1964

I. M. Parsons, ed., *Men who March Away: Poems of the First World War*, London, 1965

AUTOBIOGRAPHICAL/BIOGRAPHICAL/FICTIONAL

Richard Aldington, *Death of a Hero*, London, 1929

Henri Barbusse, *Under Fire*, London, 1917

Robert Graves, *Goodbye to All That*, London, 1929

F. M. Remarque, *All Quiet on the Western Front*, London, 1929

Frank Richards, *Old Soldiers Never Die*, London, 1933

CRITICAL

Bernard Bergonzi, *Heroes' Twilight: A Study of the Literature of the Great War*, London, 1965

John H. Johnston, *English Poetry of the First World War: A Study in the Evolution of Lyric and Narrative Form*, Princeton and London, 1964

Jon Silkin, *Out of Battle: The Poetry of the Great War*, London, 1972

HISTORICAL

A. J. P. Taylor, *The First World War/An Illustrated History*, London, 1963

Rupert Brooke

The Poetical Works of Rupert Brooke, edited by Geoffrey Keynes, London, 1970

The Letters of Rupert Brooke, edited by Geoffrey Keynes, London, 1968

Rupert Brooke/A Biography, by Christopher Hassall, London, 1964

Rupert Brooke/Four Poems, Drafts and fair copies in the author's hand with a Foreword and Introductions by Geoffrey Keynes, London, 1974

Edmund Blunden

Poems, 1914–30, London, 1930

Undertones of War, London, 1928

War Poets: 1914–1918 (The British Council and the National Book League: Writers and their Work), London, 1958

Wilfred Owen

The Collected Poems of Wilfred Owen, edited with an Introduction and Notes by C. Day Lewis and with a Memoir by Edmund Blunden, London, 1963

Wilfred Owen/War Poems and Others, edited with an Introduction and Notes by Dominic Hibberd, London, 1973

Wilfred Owen/Collected Letters, edited by Harold Owen and John Bell, London, 1967

Journey from Obscurity, by Harold Owen, 3 vols., London, 1963, 1964, 1965

Wilfred Owen, by Jon Stallworthy, London, 1974

Wilfred Owen: A Critical Study, by D. S. R. Welland, London, 1960

Isaac Rosenberg

The Collected Works, edited by Gordon Bottomley and Denys Harding, with a Foreword by Siegfried Sassoon, London, 1937

Poems, edited by Gordon Bottomley, London, 1922

Siegfried Sassoon

Collected Poems, London, 1947

Memoirs of an Infantry Officer, London, 1930

Sherston's Progress, London, 1936

Siegfried's Journey, London, 1945

Siegfried Sassoon/A Critical Study, by Michael Thorpe, Leyden and London, 1966

Edward Thomas

Collected Poems, London, 1949

Letters from Edward Thomas to Gordon Bottomley, edited by R. G. Thomas, London, 1968

Edward Thomas/A Critical Biography, by William Cooke, London, 1970

As it Was and *World Without End*, by Helen Thomas, London, 1956

© Oxford University Press 1974

ISBN 0 19 211847 1

First published 1974   Second impression 1975

Published by Oxford University Press, in association with the Imperial War Museum, London, 1974

Filmset and printed in Great Britain by

BAS Printers Limited, Wallop, Hampshire

Acknowledgements

Grateful acknowledgements are due to the following for permission to reproduce copyright material: the Trustees of the Rupert Brooke Estate for the photographs on pages 3–7 and for the manuscript of 'The Soldier'; to A. D. Peters & Co. and William Collins & Co. Ltd., publishers of *Poems of Many Years* by Edmund Blunden, for 'Vlamertinghe' and stanzas from 'Report on Experience', and to the Trustees of the Edmund Blunden Estate for the manuscript of 'Pillbox'; to the Executors of the Estate of Harold Owen and Chatto & Windus Ltd., publishers of *The Collected Poems of Wilfred Owen*, edited by C. Day Lewis, for 'The Send-off', and to the Executors of the Estate of Harold Owen for the photograph on page 13 and the manuscript of 'Anthem for Doomed Youth'; to Mr. Ian Parsons for the portrait of Isaac Rosenberg on page 18 and for the manuscript of 'Girl to Soldier on Leave'; to Mr. G. T. Sassoon and Faber & Faber Ltd., publishers of *The Collected Poems of Siegfried Sassoon*, for 'They' and 'Base Details', to Sir Geoffrey Keynes for the picture of Sassoon on page 22, and to the Trustees of the Estate of Siegfried Sassoon for the manuscript of 'The Dug-out'; to Mrs. Myfanwy Thomas and Faber & Faber Ltd., publishers of *The Collected Poems of Edward Thomas* for 'Rain' and 'In Memoriam (Easter 1915)', and to Mrs. Myfanwy Thomas for the manuscript of 'This is no case of petty right or wrong'; and to the Director and Trustees of the Imperial War Museum for the illustrations on pages 8, 9, 11, 14, 15, 17, 19, 20, 22, 23, 25, 26, 28, and 31.